Introduction

Money is a topic that many people find intimidating or overwhelming. However, mastering your money can lead to financial freedom and a more comfortable life. You can take several steps to master your money, including setting financial goals, creating a budget, managing debt, and investing wisely. This book will explore these steps in detail and provide tips and resources to help you master your money.

Table of Contents

Step 1: Set Financial Goals

The first step in mastering your money is to set financial goals. Financial goals are specific targets you want to achieve with your money, such as saving for a down payment on a home or paying off credit card debt. Setting financial goals is crucial because it gives you a clear direction and helps you stay focused on your priorities. When you set financial goals, it is helpful to follow the SMART criteria. Example: Instead of setting an unclear goal like "save more money," set a specific goal like "save $6,000 for a down payment on a home in the next 12 months." Once you have set your financial goals, tracking your progress and adjusting your plan is important. You can use tools like budgeting apps, spreadsheets, or even a simple notebook to track your progress and make adjustments along the way.

What is an example of a financial goal?
A financial goal example could be saving up a down payment for buying a house, paying off credit card debt, or creating a

retirement savings plan. Another example could be setting a specific amount of money to save each month or year for a particular financial goal, such as building an emergency fund or saving for a child's education.

What are reasonable financial goals?
There are a lot of different financial goals that people pursue depending on their individual circumstances and priorities. Here are a few examples:

1. Building an emergency fund: This is a simple saving account that you can use to accumulate funds to cover unexpected expenses, like medical bills or car repairs. Most experts recommend saving up to six months of living expenses in your emergency fund.
2. Paying off debt: This could include credit card debt, student loans, or other types of loans. Paying off debt can help you save on interest charges and improve your credit score.
3. Saving for retirement: It doesn't matter how old you are. The time to

begin saving for retirement is now. Depending on your goals and lifestyle, you should save between 10 and 20 percent of your income for retirement.

4. Down payment on a house: If you are planning to buy a home in the future, you'll need to save up a lump sum for a down payment. This could be anywhere from 3 to 20 percent of the home's purchase price.

5. Building wealth: This can mean different things to different people, but generally, it involves accumulating assets (like stocks, real estate, or businesses) that will appreciate in value over time.

Ultimately, the best financial goals for you will depend on your unique situation. It's important to consider factors like your income, expenses, debt, and future plans when setting financial goals.

What are the four types of financial goals?

There are generally four types of financial goals that people aim to achieve. These include:

1. Short-term financial goals: These goals are typically achieved within a year or less. Some Examples of short-term financial goals include paying off a credit card debt, creating an emergency fund, or saving for a vacation.

2. Intermediate financial goals: These goals take between one to five years to achieve. Examples of intermediate financial goals include buying a car, saving for a down payment on a house, or paying for a child's education.

3. Long-term financial goals: These goals take five or more years to achieve. Some Examples of long-term financial goals include saving for retirement, paying off a mortgage, or starting a business.

4. Life goals: These are financial goals that are tied to your overall life plan. Examples of life goals include achieving financial independence,

leaving a legacy for your family, or donating to a charitable cause.

By setting specific financial goals and developing a plan to achieve them, you can make steady progress toward improving your financial situation and achieving the life you desire.

This is why it is important to set financial goals.
Setting financial goals is important because it helps you establish a clear direction for your finances and provides a roadmap for achieving your desired financial outcomes. Here are some reasons why setting financial goals is important:

1. Creates a sense of purpose: Setting financial goals gives you a sense of purpose and direction. It helps you focus on what you want to achieve and motivates you to work towards it.

2. Helps prioritize spending: When you have financial goals, it becomes easier to prioritize your spending. You can identify which expenses are necessary and which ones are not and allocate your money accordingly.

3. Encourages saving: Financial goals often involve saving money for a specific purpose, such as a child's education. This encourages you to save money regularly and avoid unnecessary expenses.

4. Improves financial discipline: Setting financial goals requires discipline and commitment. By working towards your goals, you develop financial discipline, which can help you make better financial decisions in the future.

5. Provides a sense of accomplishment: Achieving financial goals provides a sense of accomplishment and satisfaction. It can boost your confidence and motivate you to set more ambitious goals in the future.

Setting financial goals is crucial for achieving financial stability and building wealth over time. It helps you identify what you want to accomplish with your money and develop a plan for getting there.

Step 2: Create a Budget

Creating a budget is essential for mastering your money. A budget is a detailed plan for how you will spend your money each month, taking into account your income, expenses, and financial goals. A budget helps you stay on track with your financial goals and avoid overspending.

To create a budget, follow the step below:

1. List all of your sources of income, such as your salary, freelance work, or rental income.
2. List your expenses, including fixed expenses like rent or mortgage payments, utilities, and car payments, as well as other variable expenses like groceries, entertainment, and travel.
3. Once you have listed your expenses and income, take away your expenses from your income to find out your net income. If you have a positive net income, you can allocate the remaining funds towards your financial goals or savings.

If you have a negative net income, you may need to adjust your spending or find ways to increase your income. There are several budgeting tools and apps available to help you create and track your budget.

Use these 5 steps to create a budget.
Creating a budget can initially seem daunting, but it's an essential step in managing your finances and achieving your goals. Here are 5 steps to help you create a budget:

1. Determine your income: One of the first steps in creating a budget is determining your total income. This includes your salary, any side hustles or freelance work, and any other sources of income.
2. List your expenses: List all your monthly expenses, such as rent/mortgage, utilities, groceries, transportation, entertainment, and any debt payments.
3. Categorize your expenses: Once you finish the list of your expenses, categorize them into fixed expenses

(such as rent or car payments) and variable expenses (such as groceries or movies).

4. Set spending limits: Based on your overall income and expenses, set spending limits for each category. Be sure to prioritize your expenses and allocate funds accordingly.
5. Track your spending: Once you have created your budget, tracking your spending is important to ensure you are sticking to your plan.
6. Use a budgeting app, spreadsheet, or pen and paper to track your expenses and adjust your budget as needed.

This is how to budget money on a low income.

Budgeting can be challenging, especially on a low income. Here are some tips for budgeting on a low income:

1. Track your expenses: Start by tracking your expenses for a month. This will help you understand where you are spending most of your money and identify areas where you can reduce spending.

2. Prioritize your expenses: Make a list of your fixed expenses, such as rent, utilities, and groceries. These are the expenses that you must pay each month. Then, prioritize your discretionary expenses, such as entertainment and dining out. Look for ways to reduce these expenses.

3. Create a budget: Once you have a good understanding of your expenses, create a budget. Allocate your income to cover your fixed expenses first, then allocate the remaining funds to your discretionary expenses.

4. Reduce your expenses: Look for ways to reduce your expenses. You can save more by cooking at home instead of eating out, using public transportation instead of owning a car, and shopping for discounted items.

5. Increase your income: You can consider taking on a side job or asking for a raise at your current job. Even a small increase in income can make a big difference.

6. Use cash: Consider using cash for your discretionary expenses. Using cash can help you avoid overspending and stay within your budget.
7. Build an emergency fund: Start setting aside a small amount of money each month to build an emergency fund. Setting aside funds will help you cover unexpected expenses without having to rely on credit cards or loans.

Remember, budgeting requires discipline and commitment. You should stick to your budget and make adjustments as necessary. Over time, you will be able to build savings and improve your financial situation.

How do you budget money for beginners?
Budgeting is an essential skill everyone should learn, especially beginners who are starting to manage their finances. Budgeting helps you track your expenses,

prioritize your spending, and achieve your financial goals.

1. Identify your expenses and all income you earn.
2. Understand your income and expenses. List down all your sources of income, including your salary, freelance work, or any other sources. Then, make a list of all your expenses, including rent, utilities, groceries, transportation, entertainment, and any other expenses you may have. Be honest and realistic about your expenses.
3. Categorize your expenses
4. Once you have listed all your expenses, categorize them into essential and non-essential expenses. Essential expenses are those that you cannot avoid, such as rent, utilities, and groceries. Non-essential expenses are those that you can live without, such as eating out or buying new clothes.
5. Set your financial goals.
6. After identifying your income and expenses, it's time to set your

financial goals. Your financial goals can be short-term or long-term, such as saving for a vacation, paying off debt, or building an emergency fund.

7. Create a budget plan. Start by allocating your income to your essential expenses first. Make sure to prioritize your bills and payments that are due soon. Then, allocate some money to your non-essential expenses, depending on your financial goals.
8. Track your expenses
9. Tracking your expenses is crucial in budgeting. It helps you monitor your spending and ensure that you are sticking to your budget plan. You can track your expenses using a spreadsheet or a budgeting app. Make sure to log every expense you make, including small purchases like coffee or snacks.
10. Review and adjust your budget.
11. Your budget plan is not set in stone. You may need to review and adjust your budget plan as your financial situation changes. For example, if you

get a raise or a promotion, you may have more money to allocate to your financial goals. On the other hand, if you encounter unexpected expenses, you may need to adjust your budget plan to accommodate them.

In conclusion, budgeting is a crucial skill that everyone should learn, especially beginners who are starting to manage their finances. Following these tips can create a budget plan that works for you and helps you achieve your financial goals. Remember to be honest and realistic about your expenses, track your spending, and adjust your budget plan as needed.

How do you make a monthly budget?
Making a monthly budget is a great way to track your finances and ensure that you are spending money wisely. Here are some steps to make a monthly budget:

1. List all of your monthly income: Start by listing all the sources of income you have in a month. This can include your salary, bonuses, freelance work, and any other sources of income.

2. Track your expenses: Next, track all of your expenses for the month. This includes everything from rent, bills, groceries, transportation, entertainment, and other miscellaneous expenses.
3. Categorize all your expenses: Once you have a list of all your expenses, categorize them into groups such as housing, utilities, food, transportation, and entertainment.
4. Set your financial goals: Determine what your financial goals are for the month. Do you want to save a certain amount of money, pay off debt, or invest in something specific?
5. Allocate funds: Allocate funds from your income to each category of expenses based on your financial goals. Make sure to prioritize essential expenses and allocate funds for savings and investments.
6. Stick to your budget: Finally, stick to your budget throughout the month. To stay on track, Keep track of your spending and adjust your budget as needed.

Following these steps will create a monthly budget that works for you and helps you achieve your financial goals.

Step 3: Manage Debt and Track your spending.

Managing debt is an important part of mastering your money. Debt can be a significant burden, both financially and emotionally. However, with a solid plan, you can pay off debt and achieve financial freedom.

To manage debt:

1. Start by listing all of your liabilities.
2. Prioritize all your debts based on interest rates and payment amounts.
3. Focus on paying off high-interest debt first, which will save you more money.

There are several strategies for paying off debt, including focusing on paying off the smallest debt first or paying off the debt with the highest interest rate first. Choose the right method that works best for you and stick to it. In addition to paying off debt, it is important to avoid taking on new debt. You should be considerate of your spending and avoid making unnecessary purchases.

This is why you need to track your spending?

Tracking your spending is crucial because it helps you understand where your money is going and where you might be overspending. By keeping a record of your expenses, you can identify areas where you can cut back and save more money. Additionally, tracking your spending can help you create a realistic budget and financial goals. It also allows you to monitor your progress toward those goals and make adjustments as needed. Without tracking your spending, it's easy to lose track of your finances and end up in a difficult financial situation.

How do I get on track with my spending?

Getting on track with your spending can be challenging, but it's not impossible. Here are the top steps that you can take to get started:

1. Create a budget - Start by tracking your spending for a month or two and categorize all your expenses. This will identify areas where you are

overspending and where you can cut back.

2. Set financial goals - Determine what you want to achieve financially, whether paying off debt, saving to make a large purchase or building an emergency fund.
3. Prioritize your spending - Once you have a budget and financial goals, prioritize your spending accordingly. Make sure you are allocating your money towards the most important things to you.
4. Use cash - Consider using cash instead of debit or credit cards for your everyday purchases. This will help keep you on track, stay within your budget, and avoid overspending.
5. Avoid impulse purchases - Before making a purchase, ask yourself if you really need the item or if it's just a want. Avoid impulse purchases and stick to your budget.

By following these steps, you can get on track with your spending and achieve your financial goals. Remember, it takes time and discipline to create new habits, but it's worth it in the long run.

How do you keep track of money on paper?

To keep track of your money, you can create a ledger or spreadsheet to record your income and expenses. You should categorize your expenses into various categories, such as housing, transportation, food, entertainment, etc. and keep track of how much you are spending in each category. You can also record your income, such as your salary or any other sources of income you may have.

In your ledger or spreadsheet, you can also include a column for the date of the transaction, the amount of the transaction, and a brief description of the transaction. This will help you to keep track of your expenses and income in a structured and organized manner.

To ensure accuracy, it is important to keep all receipts and invoices and enter them into your ledger or spreadsheet as soon as possible. This will help you to avoid any mistakes or omissions.

By keeping track of your money on paper, you can gain better insight into your spending habits and make informed decisions about your finances.

Step 4: Cut unnecessary expenses.

Cutting unnecessary expenses refers to the process of identifying and eliminating expenses that are not essential or vital to your overall financial well-being. This may involve reviewing your spending habits and finding areas where you can reduce or eliminate expenses that are not contributing to your overall financial goals. This could include things like cancelling subscriptions or memberships you no longer use, reducing your dining-out budget, or finding ways to save on utilities and other household expenses. By cutting unnecessary expenses, you can free up more money to put towards your savings, debt repayment, or other financial goals.

What does it mean to cut your expenses?
Cutting unnecessary expenses refers to the process of identifying and eliminating expenses that are not essential or vital to your overall financial well-being. This may involve reviewing your spending habits and

finding areas where you can reduce or eliminate expenses that are not contributing to your overall financial goals. This could include things like cancelling subscriptions or memberships you no longer use, reducing your dining-out budget, or finding ways to save on utilities and other household expenses. By cutting unnecessary expenses, you can free up more money to put towards your savings, debt repayment, or other financial goals.

What do you call "unnecessary expenses"? Unnecessary expenses are expenses that are not essential or required to meet basic needs or achieve important goals. These expenses may be considered frivolous or wasteful and can include things like luxury items, entertainment, or other non-essential purchases. In personal finance, it is important to differentiate between necessary and unnecessary expenses, as cutting back on unnecessary expenses can help individuals save money and achieve their financial goals more quickly.

What are three ways you can cut expenses?

There are many ways to cut expenses, but here are three effective ways:

1. Cut unnecessary subscriptions: Take a look at your credit card statements and identify any subscriptions you don't use or need. Cancel them and save that money.
2. Reduce dining out: Eating out can be a significant expense. Instead, try cooking meals at home, meal prepping, or bringing your lunch to work.
3. Negotiate bills: Call your service providers and negotiate for better rates. Many companies are willing to work with you to keep your business, which can result in lower monthly bills.

What is a reduction in unnecessary expenditure?

A reduction in unnecessary expenditure refers to the act of cutting down on expenses that are deemed unnecessary or excessive. This could involve identifying areas where money is being spent unnecessarily, such as on non-essential items, services or activities, and then taking steps to reduce or eliminate those expenditures. The aim of such a reduction is to save money, improve financial stability, and ensure that your money is being used in the most effective way possible. This can be done by setting budgets, tracking expenses, conducting regular reviews of spending habits and making changes where necessary.

Step 5: Increase your income.

Increasing your income can be a challenging task, but there are several proven strategies that you can employ to achieve this goal. These strategies include:

1. Negotiate for a salary Increase: One of the top ways to increase your income is to renegotiate your salary. If you believe that you are underpaid, you can schedule a meeting with your boss and present your case. You can also do some research to find out the average salary for your position and use this as leverage during the negotiation.

2. Start a side hustle: This can be anything from freelancing to selling products online. The key is to find something that you enjoy, and that can generate additional income.

3. Invest in yourself: Investing in yourself can also help to increase your income. This may involve taking courses or attending seminars to improve your skills or learning a new skill altogether. By investing in

yourself, you can become more valuable to your employer or clients, which can lead to higher pay.

4. Look for opportunities for advancement: If you are currently employed, look for opportunities for advancement within your organization. This may involve taking on additional responsibilities or seeking promotions. By advancing in your career, you can increase your income and gain more job security.

5. Consider a career change: If you are not satisfied with your current income, you may want to consider a career change. This can be a difficult decision, but it may be necessary to achieve your financial goals. Look for industries that are growing and in demand and consider acquiring the necessary skills to make the switch.

In conclusion, increasing your income requires effort and determination. By negotiating your salary, starting a side hustle, investing in yourself, looking for opportunities for advancement, and considering a career change, you can take steps toward achieving your financial goals.

Conclusion:

Mastering your money takes time and effort, but it is worth it in the long run. By setting financial goals, creating a budget, managing debt, and investing wisely, you can achieve financial freedom and live a more comfortable life. Remember to track your progress and adjust your plan as needed. With dedication and discipline, you can master your money and achieve your financial goals.

Each person's finances are different, and they should seek independent financial advice from a professional. Therefore, the book information does not serve as financial advice and should not be relied upon to be accurate and complete.

This page was left blank for you to make notes.

This page was left blank for you to make notes.

This page was left blank for you to make notes.

This page was left blank for you to make notes.

This page was left blank for you to make notes.

This page was left blank for you to make notes.

This page was left blank for you to make notes.

This page was left blank for you to make notes.

This page was left blank for you to make notes.

Thank you for reading